A NOTE TO PARENT

Reading Aloud with Your Child

Research shows that reading books aloud is the single most valuable support parents can provide in helping children learn to read.

- Be a ham! The more enthusiasm you display, the more your child will enjoy the book.
- Run your finger underneath the words as you read to signal that the print carries the story.
- Leave time for examining the illustrations more closely; encourage your child to find things in the pictures.
- Invite your youngster to join in whenever there's a repeated phrase in the text.
- Link up events in the book with similar events in your child's life.
- If your child asks a question, stop and answer it. The book can be a means to learning more about your child's thoughts.

Listening to Your Child Read Aloud

The support of your attention and praise is absolutely crucial to your child's continuing efforts to learn to read.

- If your child is learning to read and asks for a word, give it immediately so that the meaning of the story is not interrupted. DO NOT ask your child to sound out the word.
- On the other hand, if your child initiates the act of sounding out, don't intervene.
- If your child is reading along and makes what is called a miscue, listen for the sense of the miscue. If the word "road" is substituted for the word "street," for instance, no meaning is lost. Don't stop the reading for a correction.
- If the miscue makes no sense (for example, "horse" for "house"), ask your child to reread the sentence because you're not sure you understand what's just been read.
- Above all else, enjoy your child's growing command of print and make sure you give lots of praise. *You are your child's first teacher — and the most important one. Praise from you is critical for further risk-taking and learning.*

— Priscilla Lynch
Ph.D, New York University
Educational Consultant

For Timothy, with love from Granny
—F.M.

For Allison, Blaise, Carly, Douglas,
Emily, and Zak
—C.S.

ISBN 0-590-22859-5

Text copyright © 1996 by Faith McNulty.
Illustrations copyright © 1996 by Carol Schwartz.
All rights reserved. Published by Scholastic Inc.
HELLO READER!, CARTWHEEL BOOKS, and the CARTWHEEL BOOKS logo
are registered trademarks of Scholastic Inc.

Library of Congress Cataloging-in-Publication Data available.

20 19 18 17 16   0 1/0

Printed in the U.S.A.   23

First Scholastic printing, April 1996

Endangered
Animals

by Faith McNulty
Illustrated by Carol Schwartz

Hello Reader! — Level 3

SCHOLASTIC INC.
New York Toronto London Auckland Sydney

Cartwheel
·B·O·O·K·S·®

People and animals
share the same earth.
They have shared it for
a long, long time.

Once there was enough
of everything.
Enough food and water...

enough forest . . .

and jungle . . .

and grassy plain
for all the animals
and all the people
to share.

But the number
of people is growing.
More people need more space.
Our cities and roads,
our fields and factories . . .

and our houses
are spreading all over
the earth.

For some kinds of animals,
there is very little space left.
Some kinds of animals
may disappear.
We call them "endangered species."
Macaws . . .

and pandas . . .

gorillas . . .

grizzly bears . . .

elephants and tigers . . .

blue whales . . .

and large copper butterflies.

These are just a few
of the species
that are in danger.
All these animals need
a homeland that suits them—
where they can be safe
to live their lives
and raise their young.

If we take away too much
of their land, the day will come
when there are no more
of these species alive.
We call that "extinction."
The quagga, a horse that
lived in Africa, is extinct.

QUAGGA

The dodo, a big bird that couldn't fly, is also extinct. In the past, few people cared when a species became extinct. Now many people care.

DODO

Endangered animals need our help.
Endangered animals need laws
to protect them from hunters

and other dangers and to protect the forests and jungles and other wild places.

To save a homeland for animals,
people must give up things
we want for ourselves.

When enough people want to do that,
wild animals will no longer be in danger.

When we save a homeland
for animals, we also save
something wonderful for ourselves—
the beautiful natural world.